D1799655

THE DOOR IN THE WALL

by
Marguerite De Angeli

Student Packet

Written by
Gloria Levine

Contains masters for:

3	Pre-reading Activities
10	Vocabulary Activities
1	Study Guide
2	Critical Thinking Activities
1	Culinary Activity
2	Literary Analysis Activities
1	Crossword Puzzle
2	Writing Activities
1	Review Crossword
2	Comprehension Quizzes (Average and Advanced)
2	Unit Exams (Average and Advanced)
PLUS	Detailed Answer Key

Note

The text used to prepare this guide was the Dell Yearling softcover published by Dell Publishing, ©1949 and ©1977 by Marguerite de Angeli. The page references may differ in the hardcover or other paperback editions.

Please note: Please assess the appropriateness of this book for the age level and maturity of your students prior to reading and discussing it with your class.

ISBN 1-56137-524-1

Copyright infringement is a violation of Federal Law.

© 2000, 2004 by Novel Units, Inc., Bulverde, Texas. All rights reserved. No part of this publication may be reproduced, translated, stored in a retrieval system, or transmitted in any way or by any means (electronic, mechanical, photocopying, recording, or otherwise) without prior written permission from Novel Units, Inc.

Photocopying of student worksheets by a classroom teacher at a non-profit school who has purchased this publication for his/her own class is permissible. Reproduction of any part of this publication for an entire school or for a school system, by for-profit institutions and tutoring centers, or for commercial sale is strictly prohibited.

Novel Units is a registered trademark of Novel Units, Inc. Printed in the United States of America.

To order, contact your local school supply store, or—

Novel Units, Inc.
P.O. Box 97
Bulverde, TX 78163-0097

Web site: www.educyberstor.com

Directions: Rate the following statements before you read the story. Compare and discuss your ratings with a partner. After you have completed the novel, discuss the ratings again in light of the story.

1————— 2 ————— 3 ————— 4 ————— 5 ————— 6

agree strongly   strongly disagree

	Before	After
1. I wouldn't have wanted to live during the Middle Ages.	_____	_____
2. The "Dark Ages" were a terrible time during which civilization ceased to develop.	_____	_____
3. Ideas changed very little during the ten centuries covered by the Middle Ages.	_____	_____
4. It is too bad that the feudalism of the Middle Ages is dead.	_____	_____
5. I would have enjoyed listening to the traveling minstrels.	_____	_____
6. The code of chivalry that developed during the Middle Ages is alive and well today.	_____	_____
7. I cannot understand why so many chose a life of monasticism during the Middle Ages.	_____	_____
8. Some people were born to lead and others were born to serve.	_____	_____
9. I would rather lose the use of my legs than lose my hearing.	_____	_____
10. With regard to problems in life: "If you follow the wall far enough, there will be a door in it."	_____	_____
11. If I were living during the Middle Ages, I would rather fight in battle than live the life of a monk.	_____	_____
12. No one understands what it is like to be disabled unless he or she has experienced it.	_____	_____
13. If your hands are busy, time passes more quickly.	_____	_____
14. It is better to have crooked legs than a crooked spirit.	_____	_____
15. Keeping busy helps the time pass quickly.	_____	_____

Directions: The story you are about to read takes place during the Middle Ages, a period from around 400 AD to 1350 AD. Imagine what it was like to live in England during that time. Then look at the list below and guess which items and activities were around during the Middle Ages. Mark these with a check. Mark those which you do NOT think were around yet with an N. Then read the story and check your predictions.

___	hide and seek	___	harps
___	piggy-back rides	___	drums
___	checkers	___	pianos
___	dolls	___	flu shots
___	hobby horses	___	eyeglasses
___	pet cats	___	diets
___	pet dogs	___	thermometers
___	pet fish	___	exercise programs
___	beer	___	crutches
___	coffee	___	wheelchairs
___	hot dogs	___	curfews
___	soup	___	police officers
___	pudding	___	electric chairs
___	popcorn	___	passports
___	Christmas carols	___	newspapers
___	ballads	___	telephones
___	rhythm and blues	___	town criers
___	country fairs	___	churches
___	amusement parks	___	schools
___	universities	___	bakeries
___	shoemakers	___	daycare centers
___	storytellers	___	bathing suits
___	farmers	___	raincoats
___	fishermen	___	socks
___	basements	___	windows
___	chimneys	___	carports
___	herb gardens	___	boats
___	bedsheets	___	waterbeds
___	paper	___	pens
___	photocopiers	___	poems

All rights reserved

Name _____

Directions: *The Door in the Wall* is an example of a **genre**, or type of literature, called *historical fiction*. Everything in the story *could* have happened—and some of it did—but the story's main characters are made up. After a class discussion of what historical fiction is, fill in the chart below. Briefly describe the settings, characters, action, and problems of realistic fiction, and how they differ from those in historical fiction.

	REALISTIC FICTION	HISTORICAL FICTION
Setting:		
Characters:		
Action:		
Problem:		
Some titles:		

All rights reserved

Directions: Write a brief answer to each study question as you read the novel at home or in class. Use the questions for review before group discussions and before your novel test.

*thought question—no right or wrong answer
**prediction—no right or wrong answer

Before Reading: ** Look at the cover and title. What do you think the story will be about? What do the clothes tell you about each of the three people in the picture? What do their expressions tell you about how they are feeling? Where do you think these three are going? Why? When and where does the story seem to be set? What is the purpose of a "door in a wall"?

Chapter 1

1. Where are Robin's father and mother?

2. Where have Robin's parents arranged to send him? Why hasn't he gotten there?

3. Who is Dame Ellen and why does she stop coming?

4. Why has Brother Luke come to Robin?

5. What is wrong with Robin?

* Close your eyes and imagine that you are watching the events in the first chapter take place—"run the movie through your mind." What do you "see"? (Some of what you see may not be described in the story.) What do you hear, smell, feel?

** When will Robin's parents find out what has happened to him? Will Robin's father survive the Scottish wars? How long will it be before Robin sees his mother again? How will Robin like life at the monastery?

Chapter 2

1. There are many sorts of people at St. Mark's, although Robin can't see them. What types of people visit the monastery?

2. Why does Brother Luke bring Robin a piece of pine and a knife?

3. How do you know Robin cannot read or write?

4. What does Geoffrey call Robin? Why?

5. Explain why Luke used to be named Chaucer and why he is now called Luke.

© Novel Units, Inc.   All rights reserved

* What did you learn about herbs that you didn't know before? See if you can find out about some herbs not mentioned on page 20 (what they are used for; what they symbolize).

* Brother Luke explains that people are named for some oddity they have or for where they live, or for what they do. If we were named that way today, what name might you have? Do you know anything about the history of your name?

** Will Robin get to be friends with Geoffrey? Will Robin become less bitter? How will Robin's parents react to having a disabled son?

Chapter 3

1. Why does Robin throw the chisel?
2. Does Brother Luke think that Robin will walk again?
3. Why does Brother Luke say that reading is "another door in the wall"?
4. What does Robin say in his letter to his father?
5. How will Robin's letter get to his father?

* Compare how you learned to read and write with Robin's reading/writing lessons.

** Do you think Robin's father will get the letter? If so, how will he respond?

Chapter 4

1. What does Robin whittle after the cross is finished? Who is it for?
2. What does Brother Hubert teach Robin?
3. Why does Brother Luke take Robin to the brook?
4. What does Brother Matthew begin to make out of oak—and Robin finish?
5. What sort of celebration is going on in the city when Brother Luke and Robin arrive?

* Do you enjoy going to fairs? How do they compare with the medieval fair described in the story?

** How long will Robin stay at the monastery?

All rights reserved

Chapter 5

1. What does the letter from Robin's father say?

2. What work must be done by the ironmonger and saddler before Robin's trip?

3. How long is the trip going to be?

4. Robin, Brother Luke and John-go-in-the-Wynd meet a peasant. Where is he going?

5. Where do the travelers plan to spend the night? How do their plans change and why?

* Have you ever gotten lost while traveling? How were the consequences different for you than they were for the travelers in the story?

** What problems will the travelers run into before they reach the castle?

Chapter 6

1. The host of the Shepherd's Bush mentions that peace is rare. Who is fighting?

2. What is the White Hart and why does the friar say that it has a "fearsome look" (page 55)?

3. What is shown on page 56?

4. Why don't the strangers succeed in robbing the travelers?

5. Why does Brother Luke leave a farthing in the barn?

* Do you think the adults showed poor judgment in deciding to stay at the White Hart? What do you think would have happened if Robin had been sleeping soundly that night?

** Will the travelers run into any other problems before they arrive at the castle? How will the travelers be received?

All rights reserved

Chapter 7

1. Who are the poor people in gowns of many colors?

2. Why does Robin want to stay awhile at Wychwood Bec?

3. What is shown on page 64?

4. Why does Robin think about Gothic churches as he prays with John and the friar (p. 65)?

5. Why is the woodsman so happy to invite the travelers to spend the night?

6. Why does Robin dread the meeting with Sir Peter?

7. How do Sir Peter and his wife treat Robin?

8. Why does Adam expect trouble to come from the north or from the west?

9. Where does John's mother live and why does he tell Robin?

10. What are Robin's duties?

11. Who is D'Ath?

   * Does Robin remind you of any characters from other stories?

  ** Will Robin ever be able to mount a horse or go hawking?

Chapter 8

1. What is John-go-in-the-Wynd helping Robin make?

2. Who is Alan-at-Gate and how does Robin get along with him?

3. Where does John go?

4. Why does the enemy choose this moment to attack?

5. How do Lady Constance, the pages, and Robin help after Adam announces that the Welsh are hammering the town gate?

   * Have you ever heard the song Robin learns on the harp, "Ca' the Yaws'"?

  ** What more can Robin do to help fend off the Welsh?

© Novel Units, Inc.   All rights reserved

Chapter 9

1. How does Robin pass the time while both sides watch and wait?
2. Why does the castle's supply of food and water get so low so fast?
3. What is Robin's plan for getting help? Who knows about it?
4. How does Robin avoid getting caught by the Welsh guard who stops him?
5. What happens when Robin gets to the cottage of John-go-in-the-Wynd's mother?
   * Excitement keeps Robin wakeful as he goes over all the things he has to remember. Have you ever lain awake doing this?
  ** What problems will Robin run into? Will Sir Fitzhugh be willing to help?

Chapter 10

1. Why do John and Robin go to the church?
2. How can John tell when it is time to ring the bell?
3. How do John and Robin know the attack is successful?
4. How is John rewarded for his part in saving the castle?
5. What is Robin working on, now that the harp is finished?
6. Who comes to the castle on Christmas Eve?
7. What do Robin's parents do when they first see him with his crutches?
8. How does the King honor Robin and how does Robin thank him?
9. Where will Robin go after the Feast of Christmas is over and who else will go along?
10. Why does the friar tell Robin at the end, "...thou has found the door in thy wall."

Nones 7	clamoring 7	vexation 7	mailed 7
solar 8	plague 8	joust 9	shire reeve 9
putrid 9	coif 9	Cockney 9	Norman 10
wheedling 10	victuals 11	grotesque 11	bosses 11
embrasure 11	carters 11	retainers 12	Vespers 12
friar 12	hospice 12	cloisters 15	pallets 15
woefully 15	tethered 16	jennet 16	frock 16
sedately 17	curfew 17	postern 17	

Directions: An analogy is a comparison.

Samples: NO is to YES as OFF is to ON. *(The word pairs are opposites.)*
HILL is to MOUNTAIN as STREAM is to RIVER. *(A hill is like a small mountain; a stream is like a small river.)*

Use words from the vocabulary list to complete the analogies, below. Create analogies for five more of the vocabulary words and give them to a partner to complete.

1. CHIHUAHUA is to DOG as _____ is to HORSE.

2. PALLETS are to BEDS as _____ are to GROCERIES.

3. ENTRANCE is to FRONT as _____ is to BACK.

4. A SHOWER is to DELUGE as a COLD is to_____.

5. BOOT is to FOOT as _____ is to HEAD.

6. REVEILLE is to MORNING as _____ is to EVENING.

7. NUN is to CONVENT as _____ is to MONASTERY.

8. ADHESIVE is to GLUED as ROPE is to _____.

9. ELATION is to SATISFACTION as _____ is to DISCONTENT.

10. JOYFULLY is to WOEFULLY as WILDLY is to _____.

11. _____ is to _____ as _____ is to _____.

12. _____ is to _____ as _____ is to _____.

13. _____ is to _____ as _____ is to _____.

14. _____ is to _____ as _____ is to _____.

15. _____ is to _____ as _____ is to _____.

All rights reserved

hawthorn 18	procession 18	devotions 18	breviary 18
pilgrims 19	almonry 19	whittle 20	mutton 20
seethed 20	awry 21	bowsprit 21	pennant 21
weathered 22	keepsake 22	proportioned 22	pumice 23
scriptorium 23	psalteries 23	illumined 23	impertinent 24

Directions: Divide into groups of four and map each of the list words together. (See the map outline below.)

Step 1:   Assign each person one part of each map. One person will find synonyms; the second will find or draw pictures or symbols; the third writes definitions; the fourth writes sentences.

Step 2:   Turn to the pages on which the words appear in the book.

Step 3:   Look at how each word is used.

Step 4:   Map each word.

Step 5:   Share your maps with other groups.

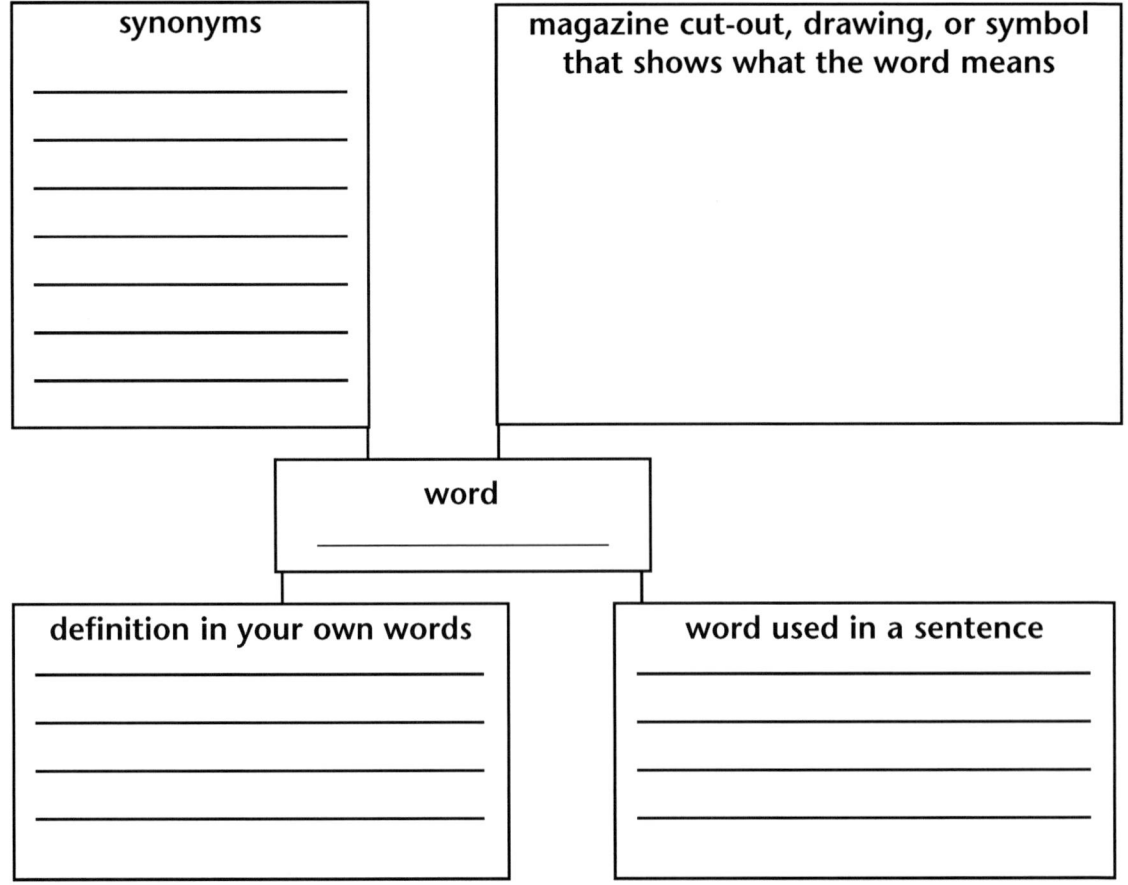

© Novel Units, Inc.   All rights reserved

abated 26	refectory 26	chapel 26	trundle cart 26
chisel 27	slivers 27	litter 27	acrid 27
plane 27	mason 28	evaporated 28	reassured 29
quill 30	parchment 30	minstrel 30	attend 31
tonsured 31	minced words 31		

Directions: Answer the following questions—

1. When a snowstorm *abates*, what does it do?

2. What would you find in a *refectory*?

3. What would a person usually do in a *chapel*?

4. How is a *trundle cart* different from a wheelbarrow?

5. What use might a person have for a *chisel*?

6. What does a *tonsured* head look like?

7. Without *mincing words*, how could you tell your parents that you flunked a test?

8. Where might you see *slivers* of wood?

9. How could a pleasant *litter* fall around you?

10. What might cause an *acrid* odor?

11. What is the purpose for the tool called a *plane*?

12. What is a *mason's* job?

13. What happens if your worries *evaporate*?

14. When was the last time someone *reassured* you?

15. What were a *quill* and *parchment* used for in the past?

16. What did a *minstrel* used to do?

17. When do you find it hard to *attend* your teachers?

© Novel Units, Inc.

All rights reserved

Name_____

Directions: Circle the word in each group that fits with the others the LEAST. Write a sentence or two explaining why the word does not belong.

1. guild   association   minstrel   club

_____

2. weir   chantry   fence   net dam

_____

3. drone   fast   clatter   peal

_____

4. habits   jerkins   crusaders   hosen

_____

5. castle   monastery   hovel   missal

_____

6. lectern   desk   pennant   table

_____

7. bosses   garlands   knobs   carvings

_____

8. legions   devotions   prayers   sins

_____

9. crookshanks   staves   ladders   casks

_____

10. mayhap   perhaps   maybe   albeit

_____

© Novel Units, Inc.
All rights reserved

Directions: Match each of the following people with the appropriate description. The words appear on the page numbers indicated. Try to guess the meaning from context and find a match before you use the dictionary.

1. verger (42) _____
2. saddler (46) _____
3. cutpurse (48) _____
4. roisterer (48) _____
5. fuller (51) _____
6. ironmonger (46) _____

a. caretaker of the church
b. person who cleanses/thickens cloth
c. noisy, boisterous type
d. pickpocket, thief
e. deals in hardware
f. person who makes horse equipment

Match each of the following words with its definition.

7. cassock (42) _____
8. cotta (42) _____
9. alternating (42) _____
10. quench (46) _____
11. pilgrimage (47) _____

12. refuge (47) _____
13. lay (47) _____
14. crook (48) _____
15. cowl (50) _____
16. galled (51) _____
17. crop (52) _____
18. brocaded (52) _____
19. punky (52) _____
20. tinder (52) _____

g. long garment worn by clergymen
h. satisfy one's thirst
i. shelter or protection from trouble
j. every other one
k. broad sleeved white vestment worn over cassock
l. graze off the tops of plants
m. curved implement
n. hooded garment worn by monks
o. woven with a raised pattern
p. made sore by rubbing
q. journey made to a sacred place
r. short poem to be sung
s. substance used to start a fire
t. dry and decayed, good for starting a fire

© Novel Units, Inc.
All rights reserved

intervals 53	heartily 54	ale 54	thatch 55
slatternly 55	noggins 56	unyielding 56	scornfully 59
louts 59	scuffling 60		

Directions: Answer the following questions—

1. What would you probably find in a *noggin*?

2. What would you probably find in a granary?

3. What would you call a mattress that is hard and has no "give"?

4. Where would you find a cottage's *thatch*?

5. How do *louts* act?

6. When do you eat *heartily*?

7. If rain falls at *intervals*, when does it fall?

8. Why might two kindergarteners be *scuffling*?

9. When was the last time you heard someone speak *scornfully*?

10. What is the difference between *ale* and ginger ale?

11. What does a *slatternly* woman look like?

© Novel Units, Inc.

All rights reserved

Directions: Match the vocabulary words on the left with their definitions.

1. ___ caparison   a. draft horse

2. ___ lombard   b. oatcake

3. ___ flagon   c. decorative horse covering

4. ___ serf   d. thick cereal or soup

5. ___ bannock   e. large drinking bottle

6. ___ newel   f. member of Northern Italian tribe

7. ___ yeoman   g. attendant in a royal household

8. ___ Percheron   h. person attached to lord's land

9. ___ hospitality   i. pillar at top of winding stairs

10. ___ ingrate   j. innermost, strongest structure of a castle

11. ___ keep   k. agents, ambassadors

12. ___ emissaries   l. variegated; different colors in different parts

13. ___ particolored   m. friendly treatment of guests

14. ___ pease porridge   n. unappreciative person

bowman 76	tracery 77	turret 78	flageolet 79
largess 79	farrier 79	tapered 79	bailey 80
portcullis 83	flambeaux 84	fripperies 84	trestles 84

A. Match each of the words above with its word history below. Then use the word in a sentence.

1. _____ from the French word "flajolet" = flute

2. _____ originally a French word meaning "generosity"

3. _____ related to the French word "ferrier" = smith

4. _____ from the French word "flambe" = flame

B. Match each of the definitions below with one of the words in the vocabulary list.

5. _____ tables with movable tops

6. _____ gradually smaller toward one end

7. _____ archer

8. _____ tower, spire

9. _____ grating at the sides of a gateway, let down to prevent passage

10. _____ fine dresses

11. _____ delicate interlacing work in carving

12. _____ courtyard surrounded by a defensive wall

catapulting 86   garrison 87   sally port 90   benedicite 91
lancers 99   drovers 99   cumber 99   priory 100
pikestaff 103   windlass 103

Directions: Complete each sentence in a way that shows you understand the meaning of the italicized word.

1. We need food because the *garrison* _____

_____.

2. The monk said, "*Benedicite*" _____

_____.

3. The company of *lancers* _____

_____.

4. When you get to the *priory* _____

_____.

5. The sentry's *pikestaff* _____

_____.

6. You might use a *windlass* to _____

_____.

7. The children were using a slingshot for *catapulting* _____

_____.

8. Go to the *sally port* _____

_____.

9. The *drovers* walked behind their _____

_____.

10. The hiker does not want to be *cumbered* by _____

_____.

sacristan 104	belfry 105	turrets 105	deliverance 106
routed 109	viol 111	banners 115	dais 118
doublet 118	realm 119		

Directions: Form a group of three and figure out the mystery words together.

Step 1: Each member of the group picks a card from the same set and reads the clue on it to the others in the group.

Step 2: Members help each other figure out the mystery word for that set of clues. (Take a look at the vocabulary list, above, only if you are stumped!)

If you were in this, you might hear a ringing in your ears.	This two-syllable word refers to a tower that is often attached to a church.	If someone says you have bats in yours, he or she thinks you're crazy.

This noun is almost a homophone for Monday, Tuesday, Wednesday, etc.	This word almost rhymes with the Spanish word for corn.	A throne might be placed on this.

This two-syllable word contains the word meaning "times two."	a close-fitting type of jacket worn during the Middle Ages	This also can refer to an undergarment worn beneath armor.

Divide the remaining words, and make clue card sets for them. Have group members try to solve your mystery clues.

© Novel Units, Inc.

All rights reserved

Here is a recipe for the "bannock" John's mother gives Robin (p. 96).

Bannocks are also known as Scottish Oatcakes. They are flat cakes made of oatmeal or barley meal and used to be baked on a hot stone; today they are made on a griddle or in an oven. The cakes are shaped into a circle and the round is cut into wedges, called farls. American oatmeal is much coarser than the oatmeal used long ago by people like John's mother, and that is why this recipe directs you to put the oats in a blender.

Bannock

1	cup quick-cooking rolled oats	$1/4$	cup hot water
2	tablespoons all-purpose flour	2	tablespoons melted butter
$1/4$	teaspoon baking powder	$1/4$	cup quick-cooking rolled oats
$1/4$	teaspoon salt		(set aside)

Place $1/2$ cup of the rolled oats in a blender and blend until the oats are a fine powder. Repeat with another $1/2$ cup of oats. Combine these with the flour, baking powder, and salt. Stir in hot water and the melted butter. Sprinkle a board with the remaining $1/4$ cup of oats. Place the dough on top. Roll to a ten-inch circle. Cut into 12 wedges. Place the wedges on an ungreased baking sheet. Bake at 350° for 15 minutes. Turn off the heat and open the oven door. Leave the bannock in the oven until firm and crisp, 4 to 5 more minutes. Serve with butter or margarine.

Note: Recipe found in *The Better Homes and Gardens Heritage Cook Book*, ©1977, ©1975.

Directions: You judge what a character is like in much the same way as you judge what a person is like in real life—by how he acts, by what he says, by what others say about him, and by what he seems to think and feel. Begin an attribute web for Robin as you start to judge what he is like at the beginning of the novel. Add to the web as you read further in the book.

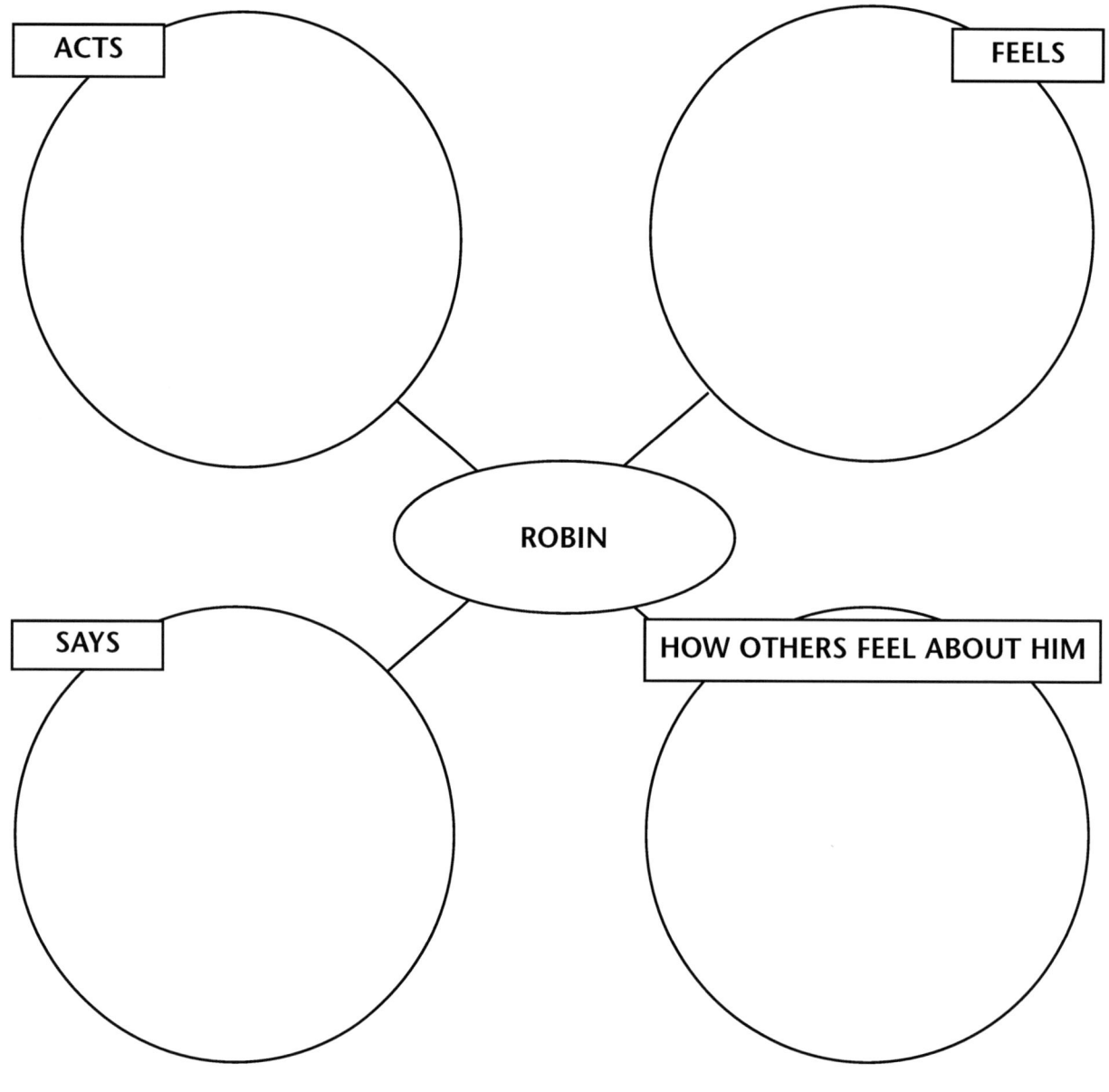

All rights reserved

Directions: With a partner, discuss Robin's decision to go for help—without telling Sir Peter. What were his reasons for going? for deciding not to tell Sir Peter?

In the YES and NO columns, write reasons why he should/should not have gone secretly for help. It is okay to write down key words and phrases rather than whole sentences. Try to include as many reasons under YES as you do for NO. Discuss your charts with another pair of partners and try to reach a consensus (agreement) on whether or not Robin made the best decision. A spokesperson for this group of four then reports the groups conclusion to the whole class.

YES	← Should Robin secretly go for help? →	NO
_____		_____
_____		_____
_____		_____
_____		_____
_____		_____
_____		_____
_____		_____

CONCLUSION:
The reason that best supports the group's conclusion is:

On a separate sheet of paper, write an essay in which you defend or criticize Robin's decision to go secretly for help.

All rights reserved

Directions: In a small group, talk about Robin's relationships with the following people: his father, Brother Luke, John go-in-the-Wynd, and Sir Peter. Act out some short scenes from the story that show how Robin got along with each of the other four characters.

Then label each arrow with a brief description of the relationship. On the arrows pointing **away** from Robin, tell how Robin feels about the character to whom the arrow is pointing. On the arrows pointing **toward** Robin, tell how each character felt toward Robin.

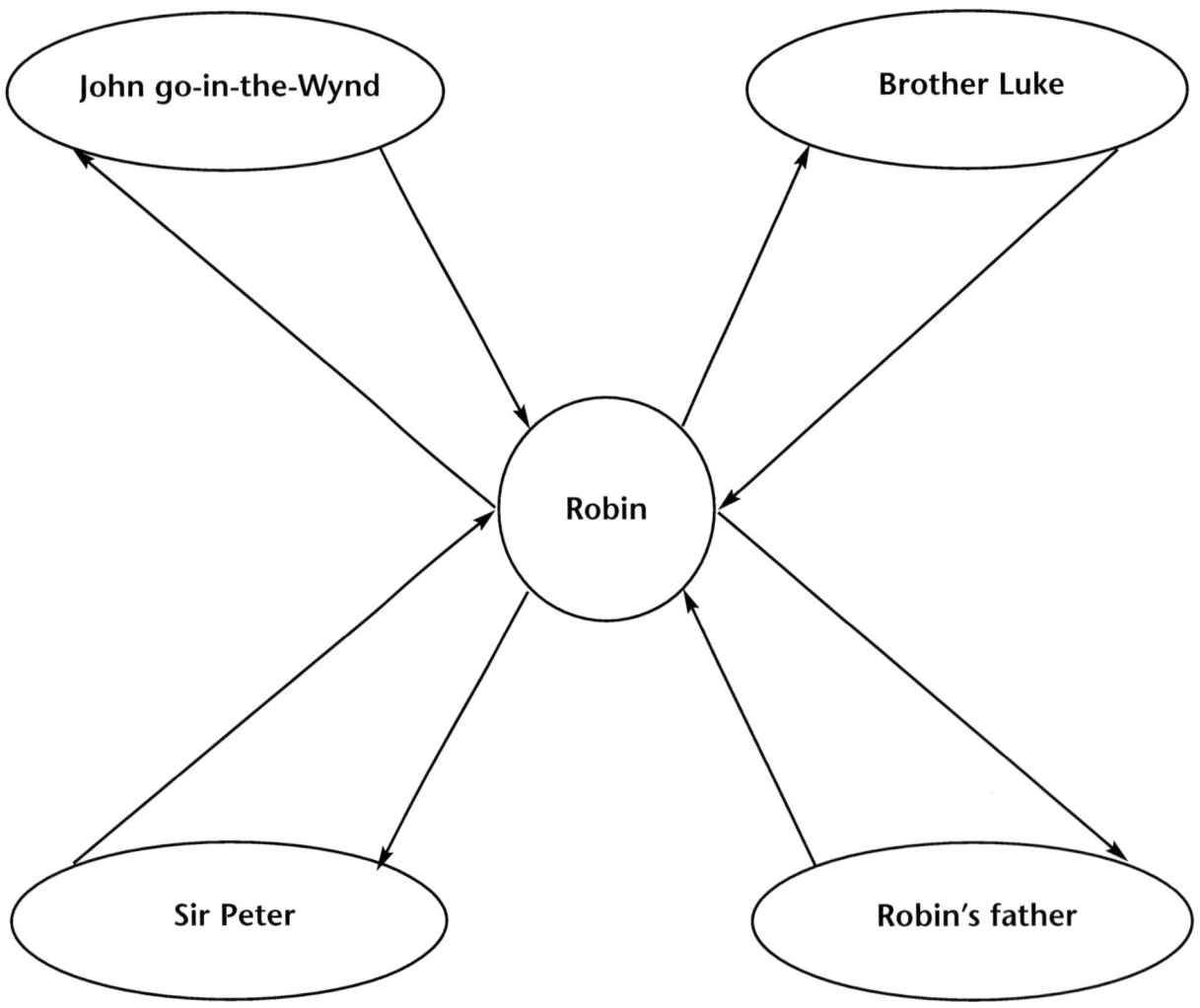

Directions: Two steps in problem solving are: (a) brainstorming possible solutions and (b) measuring each against specific criteria.

Robin faces a problem when he hears the robbers plotting in the room below. What should he do?

a) Read some of his choices in the chart below. (Add another of your own.)

b) Read the criteria. (These are questions used to decide how a particular decision "measures up.")

c) Score each choice according to each of the criteria: 1 = yes, 2 = maybe, or 3 = no.

CHOICES ↓	CRITERIA			
	Will this keep the robbers from getting suspicious?	Will this keep the robbers from getting the money bag?	Will this keep Robin safe?	Will this keep John and Luke safe?
Do nothing.				
Wake the others and leave by the window.				
Wake the others and attack the robbers.				
Wait for the robbers behind the door with a club.				
Your own idea:				

© Novel Units, Inc.

All rights reserved

Name_____

Directions: Talk about the following topics with your group. Brainstorm a list of ideas for each topic. Then: (a) choose one topic, (b) draft a composition about it, (c) read your composition to a partner, (d) revise the composition.

Ideas for this Topic

1. Robin's harp was very special to him. When the Welsh were threatening to attack, he made sure he retrieved the unfinished harp. Describe something you made that is special to you. Tell when and how you made it, and whether you still use it.

2. Robin worked long and hard on the cross, and was very frustrated when it broke. Describe a similar frustrating experience in your life.

3. It took great courage for Robin to get past the Welsh and seek help. Describe a time you did something that took courage.

4. Swimming helped Robin strengthen his body. He swam every day no matter what. Describe the kinds of exercise you get.

5. Robin was discouraged about not being able to get around on his own, until he made himself some crutches. Does this remind you of any problems you have solved?

© Novel Units, Inc.

All rights reserved

Directions: Talk with other members of your group about what the phrase "door in the wall" means. How were crutches and reading both "doors in the wall" for Robin? What other "doors" did he find? How did he feel before and after finding the "doors"? After your discussion, write a summary on the door in the wall below.

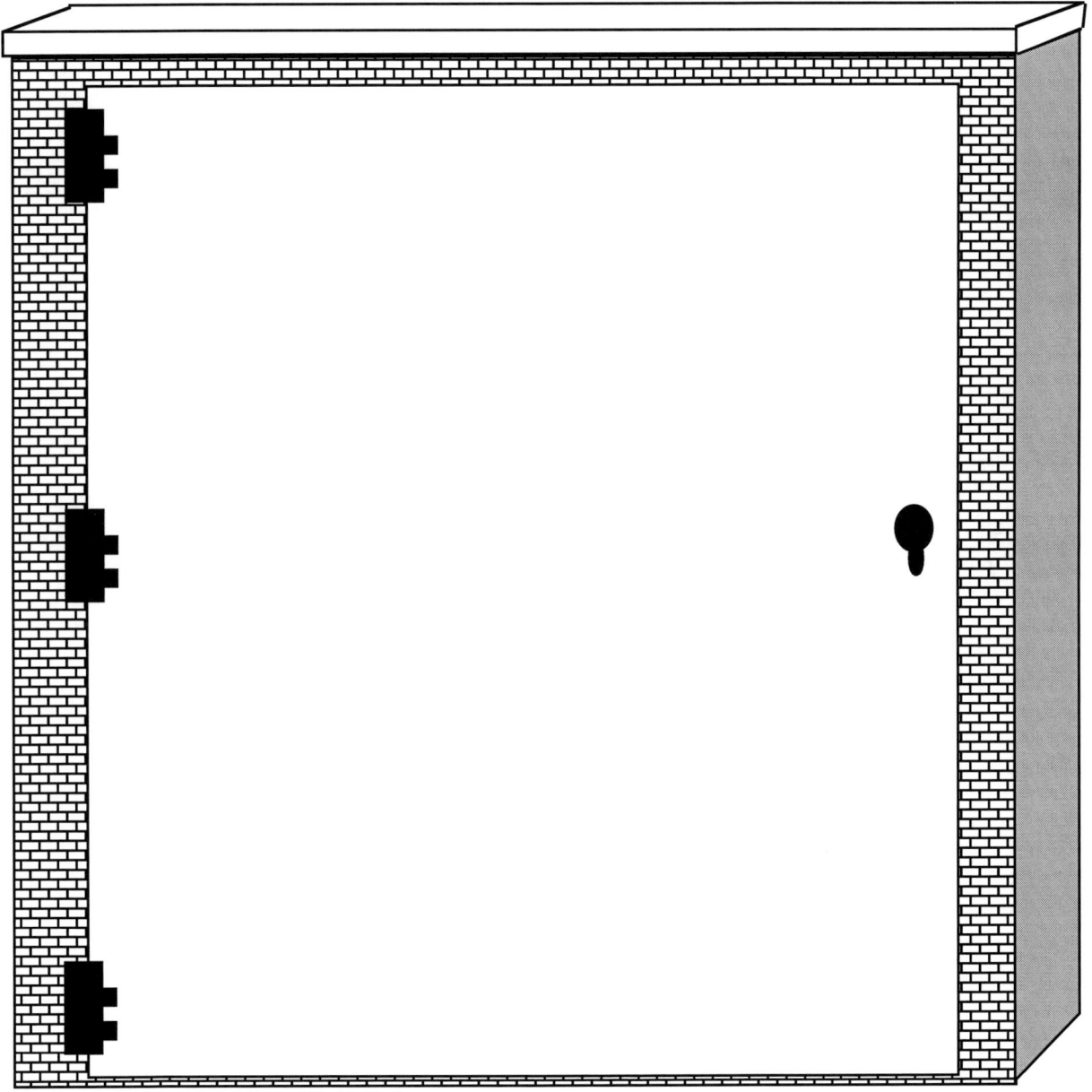

ACROSS

5. traveling singers seen at St. Mark's
7. Robin makes these to help him walk.
8. Many people died from this disease.
10. Robin plays a song of _____ for the king.
15. At the inn, Robin luckily overhears them.
17. The king gives Robin a jeweled one.
18. John is rewarded by Sir Peter with a holding of land and a portion of _____.
19. This portion of the monastery was where records and poems were copied.
22. Sir ___ agrees to help protect Sir Peter's castle, although they are not good friends.
24. Robin's mother leaves to be a lady-in-_____
26. Where Robin goes with his parents after leaving Sir Peter's castle.
29. John go-in-the-_____ brings a message from Robin's father.
30. When the travelers get lost on their way to the White Swan, Robin gets to sleep in a hollow tree _____.

DOWN

1. Robin sees some of these travelers at the monastery.
2. Another lame boy calls Robin "Brother _____."
3. Robin's father was fighting in these wars.
4. Robin watches this kind of show at the fair.
6. John and Robin enter the town through this person's house.
9. Robin enjoys learning this activity.
11. Robin is angry when this breaks.
12. Brother Luke goes with the family to be this.
13. Brother ___ takes Robin to St. Mark's.
14. Robin makes this musical instrument.
16. Bear-_____ is a popular event at the fair.
20. Robin and John sound the alarm with this.
21. This is Sir Peter's castle.
23. D'Ath is one.
24. These enemies threaten to attack Lindsay.
25. *The Door in the Wall* won this medal.
27. Brother Luke and Robin stop at this school, where the students wear particolored gowns.
28. Brother Luke encouraged Robin to do this to strengthen his limbs.

© Novel Units, Inc.

All rights reserved

Directions: Label each statement T for True or F for False. Change the false statements into true ones by rewriting them on the back of this paper.

___ 1. 10-year-old Robin gets sick and loses the use of his legs.

___ 2. Robin's father has gone off to the Scottish wars and his mother has gone off to be the queen's attendant.

___ 3. Dame Ellen takes Robin to a monastery.

___ 4. Robin finds that many people—including pilgrims, knights, merchants, and minstrels—visit the monastery.

___ 5. Brother Luke brings Robin a knife and a piece of wood in order to teach him how to start a fire.

___ 6. Robin laughs when Geoffrey Atte-Water calls him Robin-Lord-of-the-Manor.

___ 7. When spring comes, Brother Luke takes Robin into the garden where Brother Matthew shows him how to use some tools.

___ 8. When Brother Matthew criticizes the cross Robin is making, Robin throws a chisel that narrowly misses Brother Matthew's head.

___ 9. Brother Luke tells Robin that it is important to teach Robin's hands before teaching Robin's mind.

___ 10. Robin whittles a small cart for a poor boy.

___ 11. Robin learns to swim and Brother Luke takes him swimming every day.

___ 12. The monks are kind to Robin, but he doesn't make any friends among the boys.

___ 13. Robin makes himself some crutches and learns to use them.

___ 14. John go-in-the-Wynd arrives at the monastery with a letter from Robin's father.

___ 15. In the letter, Robin's father explains that Brother Luke and John-go-in-the-Wynd will accompany Robin to Shropshire.

Complete each of the following statements with a word or phrase.

16. The first night, the travelers sleep outdoors because they _____.

17. That first night of the trip, Robin is delighted to sleep in a _____.

18. The next night, they stop at a run-down _____.

19. It is a good thing that Robin does not sleep very well that night, because he _____

_____.

20. They run away and finish the night in a _____, where they leave a farthing for their "host."

All rights reserved

Directions: Fill in each blank with a word or phrase.

Robin's father goes off to the 1._____ wars and his mother leaves to be the 2._____'s lady-in waiting. Robin falls ill and is faithfully tended by Dame Ellen, until she is stricken by the 3._____. Brother Luke, a kind wandering friar, takes Robin to St. Marks, a 4._____. After a few months, Brother Luke brings Robin a knife and a piece of pine for 5._____. When Robin has finished making a little 6._____, Brother Luke brings him some pieces of walnut and suggests making a 7._____. Then he takes Robin to the scriptorium, where records, poems, and psalteries are 8._____ and promises to teach Robin to read and write. Stopping at the chapel on the way back, Robin meets a cheerful boy on 9._____ who greets Robin as "Brother 10._____." Spring comes and Brother Luke takes Robin out to the 11._____ where Brother Matthew shows him how to use some better cutting 12._____. When the chisel slips and breaks the 13._____, Robin gets angry and throws the 14._____. Seeing the boy's frustration, Brother Luke explains that they shall divide the days into teaching Robin's 15._____ and teaching his 16._____, so that he will not get so discouraged. Summer comes and Robin whittles a small 17._____ for a poor little 18._____ who lives in a hovel where Brother Luke goes on errands. While fishing with Brother Luke one day, Robin sees Geoffrey Atte-Water, and agrees with Brother Luke that he can learn to 19. _____, too. From that point on, Robin goes 20._____ every day, rain or shine. He makes friends with a group of boys, whittling a 21._____ for each, and playing outdoor games with them. After much careful work, he makes himself some 22._____ and learns to use them. A messenger, John-go-in-the-Wynd, arrives with a letter from 23. _____. 24._____ and John set out with Robin on a journey to Shropshire. At a run-down inn on the second night of the trip, Robin overhears some ruffians planning to 25._____ the travelers; Robin and his companions escape out the back window in the nick of time.

© Novel Units, Inc.

All rights reserved

Name _____

The Door in the Wall
Novel Test I
(Includes optional essay section.)

Identification: Find a character on the right who matches the description on the left. Write the letter of the character next to the matching number. Each character is to be used only once.

___ 1. He promises not to tell Brother Luke how he nearly lost his head.

___ 2. Robin's parents had arranged for him to go to this knight's household, where he would be away from the plague.

___ 3. This messenger is rewarded for his part in getting help against the Welsh.

___ 4. She tends Robin faithfully until she is stricken by plague.

___ 5. This woman, Robin's mother, assures him that it is a comfort to know that the wars will never claim him.

___ 6. This cheerful boy uses crutches and calls Robin, "Brother Crookshanks."

___ 7. This hound becomes Robin's faithful friend, following him everywhere.

___ 8. The King gives him a jeweled collar for his bravery.

___ 9. He has some differences with Sir Peter, but comes to his aid when the Welsh attack.

___10. This man, Robin's father, is a knight who rode off to the Scottish wars.

___11. He is the kind wandering friar who takes Robin to the monastery and goes with him to Sir Peter's castle.

A. Robin

B. Dame Ellen

C. Peter de Lindsay

D. Lady Maud

E. Brother Luke

F. Brother Matthew

G. John-go-in-the-Wynd

H. Geoffrey Atte-Water

I. Sir Fitzhugh

J. D'Ath

K. Sir John de Bureford

Multiple Choice: To the left of each item number, write the letter of the BEST response.

_____ 1. The story is set in

A. Wales about 300 years ago

B. the United States during the Revolutionary War

C. Scotland some time between 500 BC and 1500 BC

D. England during the Middle Ages

____ 2. While Robin is lying in bed, sick and alone, his parents think he is

    A. on his way to the Scottish Wars

    B. on his way to Sir Peter de Lindsay

    C. dying of plague

    D. safe from the plague in a monastery

____ 3. If Brother Luke hadn't taken Robin to St. Mark's, Robin probably would have

    A. died

    B. gone to the market for food

    C. written to his parents for help

    D. been taken to the castle by John-the-Fletcher

____ 4. Geoffrey calls Robin "Brother Crookshanks" because

    A. Geoffrey wants to tease Robin about his haircut

    B. Robin has told Geoffrey that is his name

    C. Robin has called Geoffrey by that name

    D. Geoffrey notices that Robin is also lame

____ 5. When Robin throws the chisel in the air, he is feeling mostly

    A. lucky

    B. spiteful

    C. elated

    D. frustrated

____ 6. Robin's father arranges for Robin to go to Sir Peter's castle with

    A. Brother Luke alone

    B. Brother Luke and Geoffrey Atte-Water

    C. Brother Luke and John go-in-the-Wynd

    D. Brother Luke and Brother Matthew

____ 7. The main reason Brother Luke encourages Robin to whittle is so that

    A. Robin's hands won't get as weak as his legs

    B. the children will have toys for Christmas

    C. Robin will be able to earn a living

    D. Robin will be doing something constructive

____ 8. Which of the following best describes Luke's attitude toward Robin's swimming?

    A. Keep it up every day rain or shine.

    B. Playing in the water is fine as long as your work is done.

    C. Sport should be pleasure and not work.

    D. Try it, but realize your limitations.

____ 9. On the way to Sir Peter's castle, the travelers sleep under the stars the first night because

    A. Robin begs to sleep outside

    B. they get lost on the way to an inn

    C. they don't trust the people in the inn they pass

    D. they are saving their money

____ 10. The second night, the travelers leave the inn during the night because Robin overhears the men downstairs planning

    A. to take their money bag

    B. to take their horse

    C. to kill them

    D. to attack the castle

____ 11. The woodsman allows the travelers to spend the night because

    A. he is a friend of Brother Luke's

    B. he is afraid they will rob him otherwise

    C. he knows that Robin is the son of a noble

    D. he is happy to return a favor

© Novel Units, Inc.

All rights reserved

_____ 12. Which of the following best describes how Robin feels as he thinks ahead to his meeting with Sir Peter?

    A. anxious about what Sir Peter will think of him now that he can't use his legs

    B. nervous because he has heard that Sir Peter is bad-tempered

    C. delighted because he has been lonely at the monastery

    D. eager because he knows that Sir Peter will have his best doctors fix Robin's legs

_____ 13. What is one of Robin's duties at Sir Peter's castle?

    A. serving at the high table

    B. helping the boys with their food

    C. teaching the boys to swim

    D. standing guard every other night

_____ 14. What does Lady Constance ask Robin to do after the announcement that the Welsh are hammering the town gate?

    A. carry food from the table

    B. care for the little boys

    C. gather all the women into the keep

    D. collect the embroidery frames and cloaks

_____ 15. What instrument is Robin making and learning to play when the Welsh attack the town?

    A. French horn

    B. violin

    C. harp

    D. drum

All rights reserved

_____ 16. As John explains how careful Robin must be to carve the keys to fit the holes in the harp, John says, "Thou canst but try. Anyone can NOT do it." In other words, John is saying

    A. No one has done it before, but you may be the first.

    B. If you try hard enough, you will succeed.

    C. I don't want to be the one to discourage you.

    D. It's better to try and fail then never to try at all.

_____ 17. Who knows about Robin's plan for going to get help?

    A. Robin tells no one

    B. only Sir Peter

    C. only Adam, Denis, and Brother Luke

    D. only Brother Luke

_____ 18. A Welsh guard does stop Robin, but luckily

    A. the guard thinks Robin is a shepherd boy

    B. Robin runs faster than the guard

    C. Robin has enough money to bribe the guard

    D. the guard knows and likes Robin

_____ 19. Right after Robin tells John-go-in-the-Wynd that the Welsh are attacking, John goes

    A. back to the castle to help defend it

    B. to ring the bell for help

    C. to get help from Robin's father

    D. to get help from Sir Fitzhugh

_____ 20. John's reward for his part in saving the castle is

    A. some land and some sheep

    B. a jeweled collar

    C. a dog

    D. a bag of gold

All rights reserved

_____ 21. The King honors Robin by giving him

    A. some land and some sheep

    B. a jeweled collar

    C. a dog

    D. a bag of gold

_____ 22. Robin's gift to the King is

    A. a harp

    B. a song

    C. a carved boat

    D. a carved cross

_____ 23. Which of the following best describes how Robin's parents feel about having a son who must use crutches?

    A. They feel sorry for him but try to hide their sorrow.

    B. Robin's father is openly disappointed that his son will not be able to ride in battle, but his mother is not.

    C. They love him and are so proud of him they hardly notice the crutches.

    D. They joke about the crutches and tell him that soon he will no longer need them.

_____ 24. When Robin learns that he will be going back to London, he feels

    A. surprised and saddened

    B. anxious but accepting

    C. disappointed and lonely

    D. relieved and happy

_____ 25. Which of the following is NOT a "door in the wall" for Robin?

    A. making his crutches

    B. learning to read

    C. learning to write

    D. breaking the cross

© Novel Units, Inc.   All rights reserved

Name _____

Written Response

Analysis—

Directions: Select A or B and indicate the letter of the question you decide to answer. Answer in one well-organized paragraph.

    A. At the end, Brother Luke tells Robin, "thou has found the door in thy wall." Explain what he means.

    B. Robin's illness resulted in a disability. He lost the use of his legs. Give at least three reasons why you do or do not agree with the following statement:

        Robin's disability helped him to grow.

Critical and Creative Thinking—

Directions: Select C or D.

    C. You are Robin, a year after the events in the story. You make a Christmas present for Brother Luke and you write him a letter thanking him for all that he has done for you. Write the letter. Mention why you made him what you did and why you feel so grateful to him.

    D. This book has been praised for the way it describes the times in which Robin lived. Tell at least three things you learned about the Middle Ages from this book. Did the story make the Middle Ages "come alive" for you?

Directions: Use separate paper to answer the questions on this test. Be sure to mark your answers clearly with the heading for each section (for example, "Identification") and the item numbers.

Identification: Explain who each character is and briefly describe him or her in one or two sentences.

1. Robin
2. Dame Ellen
3. Peter de Lindsay
4. Lady Maud
5. Brother Luke
6. Brother Matthew
7. John go-in-the-Wynd
8. Geoffrey Atte-Water
9. Sir Fitzhugh
10. D'Ath
11. Sir John de Bureford

Short Answer: Answer each question in one or two complete sentences.

1. Why did Robin sometimes wish he were the son of a carpenter instead of the son of a noble?
2. What skills did Robin develop as he recuperated at the monastery and later at the castle?
3. How did Robin help thwart the robbery attempt at the inn?
4. How did Robin prove his bravery when Sir Peter's castle was under attack?
5. What do you think would have happened to Robin if both of his parents had died in the plague?
6. Describe one time music plays a role in the story.
7. Explain how and why Robin learned to whittle and tell at least three of the objects he made.
8. What part of the story did you find most exciting?

9. Tell one thing you would like about living during Robin's time—and one thing you wouldn't like.

10. How does Robin change between the beginning of the story and the end?

11. Describe one problem faced by Robin that a 10-year-old boy would never have to face today.

12. Describe one problem faced by Robin that is still faced by 10-year-olds today.

13. Explain how Brother Luke helped Robin.

14. Explain why Robin was worried about his reunion with his parents—and whether or not their reactions showed that his worry was justified.

Essay

Analysis—
Directions: Select A or B and indicate the letter of the question you decide to answer.

A. Explain the significance of the title. Support your answer with at least three examples from the book.

B. Choose another book whose main character reminds you in some way of Robin. Perhaps the character also lives during the Middle Ages (such as Adam in *Adam of the Road* or one of the characters in *Robin Hood of Sherwood Forest*) or perhaps the character, like Robin, also has a disability (such as Colin in *The Secret Garden*). Compare and contrast these two characters.

Critical/Creative Writing—
Directions: Select C or D and indicate the letter of the question you decide to answer.

C. *The Door in the Wall* was awarded the Newbery Medal for most distinguished children's book over thirty years ago. Explain why you do or do not feel that the book deserves the Newbery Medal. Include at least three criteria for excellence that you believe the book meets (or does not meet).

D. Write a letter to Robin. Tell him about a "door in the wall" you found (or are searching for) and compare it to his experiences.

© Novel Units, Inc.

39

All rights reserved

Answer Key

Study Questions

Chapter 1: 1. His father has gone off to the Scottish Wars; his mother is serving the queen as lady-in waiting. 2. He is supposed to be on his way to Sir Peter de Lindsay with John-the-Fletcher, but John is attacked by thieves and then Robin grows sick and unable to walk. 3. She is a servant who takes care of Robin until she falls ill with the plague. 4. A widow told him that the servants had left Robin. 5. He doesn't have the plague, but has had some illness that left him unable to walk.

Chapter 2: 1. pilgrims, knights, merchants, minstrels, the poor 2. to whittle 3. The narrator tells us that "Robin wished he had known how to read" the pages Brother Luke shows him; he asks Brother Luke to teach him how to write. 4. "Brother Crookshanks"—because he notices that Robin, has legs that are lame, as Geoffrey does. 5. His father was a shoemaker; Luke took the name of a physician in the Bible when he took the vow to be a monk.

Chapter 3: 1. He is frustrated after he breaks the cross he is making. 2. He is not willing to venture a guess when asked. 3. He is trying to tell Robin that if he learns to read, he will understand new worlds, new ways of solving problems. 4. He tells how helpless he was when taken ill, how useless his legs are, and that he is in the care of the monks now. 5. A minstrel, John-go-in-the-Wynd, is going to the Scottish border along with a band of soldiers.

Chapter 4: 1. a doll for a poor little girl 2. about the stars, far-off countries, the Crusades, history 3. to fish—and with the idea that Robin might try swimming 4. crutches 5. The city is decorated for Midsummer Eve and food and drink are set out for passersby.

Chapter 5: 1. He is shocked to learn of Robin's illness, but glad it isn't plague; he won't tell Robin's mother, who is with the ailing queen; Sir Peter has been wounded and will be taken home; Robin will travel with Brother Luke and John-go-in-the-Wynd to Shropshire. 2. They need to make a chair-saddle for Robin. 3. over a hundred miles 4. to the forest of his lord's manor to gather wood for house fires 5. to an inn called the White Swan; They get lost and sleep outside instead.

Chapter 6: 1. The Welsh and Scots are fighting the English and there is conflict between the lords of the manors and the peasants. 2. The White Hart is a run-down looking inn with a slatternly goodwife. 3. The ruffians are probably eying Brother Luke's money pouch. 4. Robin hears them plotting and the travelers escape out the window. 5. to pay for having stayed there part of the night.

Chapter 7: 1. students at Oxford 2. He wants to see the fair. 3. Punch and Judy puppet show at the fair 4. The trees arch overhead like the roof of a cathedral. 5. Earlier John helped the woodman bind a wound he'd gotten from a fallen ax and carried him home. 6. He doesn't know how Sir Peter will react to his crutches. 7. They are warm in their welcome and seem not to notice that Robin cannot straighten. 8. Lord Jocelyn to the west wants Sir Peter's domain and Sir Hugh Fitzhugh to the north has a quarrel with Sir Peter. 9. She lives near the village by the church; John is staying with his mother and probably wants Robin to know the way in case John is needed—or Robin wants to visit. 10. learn to shoot a bow and arrow, study Latin, help the boys with their food, see that his lady is well looked after 11. One of the hounds, he follows Robin everywhere.

Chapter 8: 1. a harp 2. a sentry; Robin gives Alan the honey cakes he likes. 3. to his mother's cottage 4. A fog has rolled in. 5. Lady Constance tells Robin to care for the boys while she and her ladies gather embroidery frames and clothes, and the pages carry the food and table boards to the keep.

Chapter 9: 1. mostly working on his harp 2. Many townspeople have come to the castle for protection; fish haven't been plentiful; the sheep haven't been slaughtered yet; the flour from the peasants' holdings hasn't been brought to the castle yet. 3. He tells one of the pages and Brother Luke and Adam that he is going for help—perhaps from Sir Fitzhugh (who is a cousin of Sir Peter's, even if the two aren't on the best of terms). He will begin by going to see John at his mother's cottage. 4. He pretends to be a shepherd boy on the way home. 5. He tells John about the attack by the Welsh, and John hurries off for help while John's mother feeds Robin and puts him to bed.

Chapter 10: 1. to ring the bell as a signal that Sir Fitzhugh's forces should move in about the town and castle wall 2. He has agreed to wait an hour after curfew; he plays two songs that he knows take about a half hour so that he can sense how much time is passing. 3. They can see the company of Sir Fitzhugh's men enter and take the town, and watch as the Welsh are marched out. 4. with some land and sheep 5. making a violin 6. the King and Queen and Robin's parents 7. Both parents hug him and nothing is said of his legs. 8. The King gives Robin a jeweled collar and praises him for his courage; Robin plays a Christmas song on the harp and sings. 9. He will go to London with his parents and with Brother Luke as a tutor. 10. No longer will Robin be separated from his parents or worried about his disability; his troubles have come to an end.

Activities

Students should be allowed to discuss open-ended activities such as **Activity #1** (opinions) and **Activity #2** (predictions) which have no "right" or "wrong" answers.

Activity #3:

	REALISTIC FICTION	HISTORICAL FICTION
Setting:	our world, past or present	our world, sometime in the past
Characters:	like us	like real people of the time; real figures from history are mentioned and sometimes
Action:	could happen, but is not a true story	some of the story did not happen, some of it might have happened, and all of it could have happened; not an entirely true story, but sounds like one
Problems:	realistic	like those of the people living in that time
Some titles:	*Bridge to Terabithia, Hatchet, The Outsiders*	*Sign of the Beaver, Island of the Blue Dolphins, The Witch of Blackbird Pond*

Activity #4: 1-jennet; 2-victuals; 3-postern; 4-plague; 5-coif; 6-curfew; 7-friar; 8-tethered; 9-vexation; 10-sedately; 11-15 will vary

Activity #5: Maps will vary, and should be shared so that all words are covered.

Activity #6: Sample answers: 1. it lets up; 2. dining tables, food; 3. pray; 4. wagon with four wheels, not one; 5. chipping stone or wood, as when carving a statue; 6. The crown is shaved. 7. by telling them flatly and directly; 8. around a carpenter's bench; 9. if the bits of waste were composed of something pretty, like confetti; 10. burning rubber; 11. smoothing wood; 12. building with stones or bricks; 13. They go away. 14. Students should mention a time they were anxious and someone encouraged them. 15. pen and paper for writing; 16. sang or recited to entertain others; 17. when they speak in a monotone

Activity #7: Sample answers: 1. minstrel; Minstrels are wandering singers while the rest are organizations. 2. chantry; A chantry is a chapel for singing and minor services while the others are all types of restraining structures. 3. fast; Fasting is not eating while the others are all sounds. 4. crusaders; Crusaders were Christians trying to recover the Holy Land from the Muslims while the rest are clothes. 5. missal; A missal is a prayer book while the rest are buildings. 6. pennant; The others are types of furniture. 7. garlands; A garland is a wreath of flowers while the rest are architectural ornaments. 8. legions; Legions are units of soldiers while the rest have to do with religion. 9. crookshanks; Crookshanks are crooked legs while the rest refer to narrow pieces of wood and the objects made from them. 10. albeit; Albeit means "although" while the others all mean "maybe."

Activity #8: a-1, b-5, c-4, d-3, e-6, f-2, g-7, h-10, i-12, j-9, k-8, l-17, m-14, n-15, o-18, p-16, q-11, r-13, s-20, t-19

Activity #9: Sample answers: 1. ale; 2. grain-oats, corn; 3. unyielding; 4. on the roof; 5. boorish and rude; 6. when you are hungry or trying to show your appreciation of someone else's cooking;

© Novel Units, Inc.

All rights reserved

7. on and off; 8. because of a disagreement over a marker; 9. Students mention the last time someone spoke in a mocking or skeptical way. 10. Ale is alcoholic while ginger ale is a soft drink. 11. sloppy, untidy, uncombed

Activity #10: 1-c; 2-f; 3-e; 4-h; 5-b; 6-i; 7-g; 8-a; 9-m; 10-n; 11-j; 12-k; 13-l; 14-d

Activity #11: A. 1-flageolet; 2-largess; 3-farrier; 4-flambeaux; B. 5-trestles; 6-tapered; 7-bowman; 8-turret; 9-portcullis; 10-fripperies; 11-tracery; 12-bailey

Activity #12: Answers should be sentences that reflect an understanding of the following definitions: 1-garrison—body of troops stationed in a fortified place; 2-Benedicite—a blessing; 3-lancers—mounted soldiers armed with shafted weapons; 4-priory—religious house governed by a prior or prioress; 5-pikestaff—staff or long stick with a spike at the lower end; 6-windlass—hauling device consisting of a barrel turned by a crank; 7-catapulting—hurling; 8-sally port—gateway permitting the passage of a large number of troops at a time; 9-drovers—those who drive cattle, sheep, etc. to market 10-cumbered—encumbered, overloaded, obstructed

Activity #13: 1-belfry; 2-dais; 3-doublet

Activity #15: Webs will vary, but should reflect the fact that Robin at first acts rather pompous toward Dame Ellen, misses his parents, feels self-pitying, is pitied by some of the adults around him like Dame Ellen. As the story progresses, Robin becomes more cheerful, self-sufficient, concerned about the welfare of others.

Activity #16: Answers will vary. Sample answers: No—He is putting himself in danger; he is going behind his host's back; perhaps Sir Peter could help; Yes—Somebody has to do it; if Robin told Sir Peter, Sir Peter might not allow him to go; Robin is more likely to get by the guards than others who are older.

Activity #17: Answers will vary but should reflect the fact that Brother Luke is Robin's patient teacher who thinks highly of Robin's ability to help himself and Robin respects Brother Luke; John helps Robin get to Sir Peter's, shows him how to make a harp, helps him get aid in fighting the Welsh; Robin respects and admires John; Sir Peter is supportive of Robin, telling him that everyone has a place in the world; Robin respects and admires Sir Peter; Robin's father has high expectations for his son but is reassuring and supportive; Robin wants his father to be proud of him.

Activity #18: Answers will vary; most will agree that leaving by the window was the safest option for all.

Comprehension Quiz—correcting true-false

1-T; 2-T; 3-F—Dame Ellen brings food to Robin and cares for him; Brother Luke takes Robin to a monastery. 4-T; 5-F—to teach him how to whittle; 6-F—Robin gets irritated when Geoffrey calls him Brother Crookshanks. 7-T; 8-F—It is when the cross breaks that Robin throws the chisel. 9-F—Brother Luke says that it is important to

---

© Novel Units, Inc.

All rights reserved

teach both the hands and the mind. 10-F—Robin whittles a doll for a poor girl. 11-T; 12-F—Robin befriends several boys and carves boats for them.
13-T; 14-T; 15-T; 16-lose their way to the inn; 17-tree trunk; 18-inn; 19-overhears robbers planning to attack the group; 20-barn

Comprehension Quiz—completion (Accept other defensible answers.)
1-Scottish; 2-queen; 3-plague; 4-monastery; 5-whittling; 6-boat; 7-cross; 8-copied; 9-crutches; 10-Crookshanks; 11-garden; 12-tools; 13-cross; 14-chisel; 15-mind; 16-hands; 17-doll; 18-girl; 19-swim; 20-swimming; 21-boat; 22-crutches; 23-Robin's father; 24-Brother Luke; 25-rob

Novel Test I

Identification: 1-F; 2-C; 3-G; 4-B; 5-D; 6-H; 7-J; 8-A; 9-I; 10-K; 11-E
Multiple Choice: 1-D; 2-B; 3-A; 4-D; 5-D; 6-C; 7-D; 8-A; 9-B; 10-A; 11-D; 12-A; 13-B; 14-B; 15-C; 16-D; 17-C; 18-A; 19-D; 20-A; 21-B; 22-B; 23-C; 24-D; 25-D
Written Response: (Answers might contain these details. Others may be acceptable.)
A. Robin's separation from his parents is over and he has learned to be self-sufficient despite his disability. B. He learned—to handle frustration better—to make beautiful things with his hands—not to expect others to do everything for him—to find the courage to risk his life for others. C. Robin might make something like a cart for Brother Luke to use on his visits to the homes of the poor. Robin might thank Brother Luke for going to him when he was ill, teaching him to read and write, helping him learn to swim, traveling with him to Sir Peter's and later to London to be his tutor. D. The book describes the different parts of a castle, the many conflicts (e.g., the Scottish wars, conflicts between the English and the Welsh, between peasants and landlords), the types of travelers that passed through monasteries, what a medieval fair was like.

Novel Test II

Identification: 1. Robin is a ten-year-old boy, son of a noble, the main character of the story who loses the use of his legs and bravely goes for help when the castle is surrounded by the Welsh.
2. Dame Ellen is the kind, poor servant who takes food to Robin when he is ill—porridge which he throws at her. 3. Peter de Lindsay is the knight who is supposed to teach Robin the ways of knighthood. He is injured in battle and greets Robin warmly when Robin eventually does come to his castle. 4. Lady Maud is Robin's mother and the queen's lady-in-waiting. She hugs him after their separation and reassures him about his legs, telling him she is glad she doesn't have to worry about his going off to war. 5. Brother Luke is the kind traveling friar who goes to Robin when he is sick and takes him to the monastery where he teaches him to read and write and many other things. 6. Brother Matthew is one of the monks to whom Brother Luke introduces Robin. Brother Matthew teaches Robin how to use several tools and jokes when Robin throws the chisel. 7. John go-in-the-Wynd is a messenger who delivers letters between Robin and his father, accompanies Robin to the castle, and goes for help when the Welsh attack. 8. Geoffrey Atte-Water is a boy who uses crutches and irritates Robin at first by calling him "Brother Crookshanks." 9. Sir Fitzhugh is a relative of Sir Peter's who puts aside their differences when he sends soldiers to defend Sir Peter's castle. 10. D'Ath is the hound who follows Robin everywhere. 11. Sir John de Bureford is Robin's father, a nobleman who went to fight in the Scottish wars.

Short Answer: 1. Then he wouldn't have to worry about learning the skills and assuming the responsibilities of a noble. 2. whittling, carpentry, swimming, archery 3. He woke Brother Luke and they both woke John, then climbed out the window. 4. He left the castle, swam in a cold, powerful current, and got past enemy soldiers in order to get help. 5. Answers will vary. With Brother Luke's encouragement, Robin might have found a "door in the wall" of grief, then later been adopted by Sir Peter. 6. Sample: John played a signal on his harp, recognized by the shoemaker who let them in. 7. Brother Luke showed him how so that he would have something to do with his hands; he made

boats, a cross, a doll. 8. Answers will vary; perhaps the scene where Robin left the castle to get help against the Welsh. 9. Sample: Students might like to see a medieval fair, might not like to have to face the risk of plague. 10. At the beginning he is self-concerned and dependent on others; by the end he is more self-sufficient, concerned about the feelings and welfare of others. 11. plague 12. making friends 13. Brother Luke provided for Robin's physical needs—food, massaging his legs, a place to stay in the monastery, helped him learn to read and write, helped teach him patience and hope.
14. He was worried that they would think less of him because he was on crutches. They both embraced him warmly and disregarded the crutches.

Essays: (might include these details)
A. Most problems have solutions; most bleak times get better. Robin learns to use crutches, to read and write, to make himself useful at the castle, and is reunited with his parents. B. Like Colin, Robin is from one of the upper classes and at first expects to be served, treats servants arrogantly. Like Colin, Robin learns new skills and becomes more aware of others. Unlike Colin, Robin doesn't learn to walk without support (at least during the story). C. The setting is full of authentic detail; the plot is full of action; the characters are believable; the story teaches a moral lesson without moralizing.
D. Answers will vary. The letter should tell about how the student solved a problem or developed an attitude/philosophy that helped in handling a problem.